NATURAL W

DOLPHIN

HABITATS • LIFE CYCLES • FOOD CHAINS • THREATS

Nic Davies

HODDER
Wayland

an imprint of Hodder
Children's Books

Produced in Association with WWF-UK

NATURAL WORLD

Chimpanzee • Crocodile • Black Rhino • Dolphin • Elephant
Giant Panda • Giraffe • Golden Eagle • Great White Shark
Grizzly Bear • Hippopotamus • Killer Whale • Leopard • Lion
Orangutan • Penguin • Polar Bear • Tiger

Produced for Hodder Wayland by
Roger Coote Publishing
Gissing's Farm, Fressingfield
Suffolk IP21 5SH, UK

WWF is a registered charity no. 1081247
WWF-UK, Panda House, Weyside Park
Godalming, Surrey GU7 1XR

Cover: Eye to eye with a bottlenose dolphin.
Title page: A dolphin gives the camera a friendly glance.
Contents page: This dolphin is using its tail to rise above the waves.
Index page: A pair of dolphins swimming off the coast of the Bahamas.

Editor: Steve Setford
Series editor: Polly Goodman
Designer: Sarah Crouch
Cover designer: Victoria Webb

Published in Great Britain in 2000 by Hodder Wayland,
an imprint of Hodder Children's Books
First published in paperback in 2001
Reprinted in 2002

A Catalogue record for this book is available from the
British Library.

ISBN 0 7502 2745 1

Printed in Hong Kong by Wing King Tong

Hodder Children's Books
A division of Hodder Headline Ltd
338 Euston Road, London NW1 3BH

Picture acknowledgements
Bruce Coleman 7 (Ken Balcomb), 12 (Carl
Roessler), 16 (Jeff Foott), 22 (Jane Burton), 48 (Jeff
Foott); Nic Davies 35; Digital Vision 39, 40, 41;
FLPA/Earthviews *front cover*; NHPA 6 (Roger
Tidman), 8 (Laurie Campbell), 10 (Gerard Lacz), 26
(Norbert Wu), 29 (Gerard Lacz), 30 (Norbert Wu),
32 (Kelvin Aitken); Oxford Scientific Films 13, 14
(Konrad Wothe), 15 (Daniel J. Cox), 20 (Kim
Westerskov), 33 (D.G. Fox), 34 (Kathie Atkinson),
36 (David B. Fleetham), 43, 44 middle, 45 bottom
(Konrad Wothe). Science Photo Library 37
(Dolphin Institute); Still Pictures 1 (Robert Henno),
17 (Horst Schafer), 19, 21 (Roland Seitre), 28 (H.
Ausloos), 38 (M. and C. Denis-Hoot), 42 (Mark
Carwardine), 44 bottom (Host Schafer), 45 top (H.
Ausloos); The Stock Market 11 (Craig Tuttle) 18;
Tony Stone 3 (Tim Davis); Tom Walmsley 9, 27, 31,
44 top. Map on page 4 by Victoria Webb. All other
artworks by Michael Posen.

Contents

Meet the Dolphin

Dolphins are air-breathing mammals, just like us, but they spend their entire lives in water. There are many different species of dolphin, and millions of individuals. Dolphins live in oceans, seas, lakes and rivers throughout the world, usually in groups called schools, herds or pods.
The most popular of all dolphins is the bottlenose, which is famous for its friendliness towards people. It is also the dolphin most commonly kept in marine zoos.

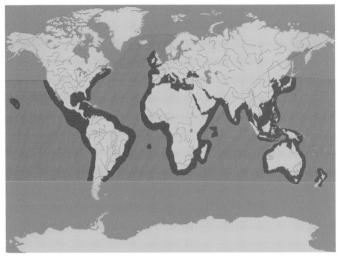

▲ The bright-red shading on this map shows where most bottlenose dolphins live. They also live in the brown shaded areas, but in much smaller numbers.

DOLPHIN FACTS

The bottlenose dolphin got its name because the shape of its beak reminded people of old-fashioned bottles. It also has a scientific name, which is *Tursiops truncatus*.

●

Males grow slightly larger than females and can reach 4.1 metres in length and weigh 650 kilograms.

▶ An adult bottlenose dolphin leaping from the water.

Dorsal fin
This hook-shaped, boneless fin acts like the keel of a boat, helping to prevent the dolphin rolling in the water.

Skin
The smooth skin is very sensitive. It secretes an oily substance, which may help the dolphin to move through the water more easily.

Blowhole
This is the dolphin's nostril. It is sealed with a muscular flap of skin to keep out water when not taking a breath.

Melon
This fatty bulge in the forehead helps to focus the sounds the dolphin uses to hunt and communicate.

Body
The torpedo-shaped body, more than one-third of which is muscle, gives the dolphin a smooth swimming action.

Beak
The bottlenose's beak, or snout, is shorter than in many other dolphin species.

Flippers (pectoral fins)
These are used for steering and communicating by touch.

Eyes
Each eye can move independently, giving excellent all-round vision both above and below the surface.

Tail
The tail, with its two boneless fins called flukes, is used for swimming. It is moved up and down, not from side to side like a fish's tail.

Blubber
Below the skin is a layer of fat called blubber, which keeps the cold out and acts as an energy store.

A humpback whale feeds by taking a huge gulp of water and then pushing it out through its horny baleen plates to sieve out food.

▼ Orcas are toothed cetaceans that hunt a wide variety of sea animals, including seals, dolphins, whales, penguins, and squid.

The Cetacean Family

Dolphins and their close cousins, the whales and porpoises, are together known as cetaceans (pronounced 'sir-tay-shuns'). This family of aquatic mammals includes the largest animal on Earth – the mighty blue whale, which can reach 31 metres long and weigh 200 tonnes.

Scientists have discovered 81 cetacean species, but there are probably more. Of these, 35 are true dolphins, including the largest dolphin, the orca (also known as the killer whale). Some dolphins live in family groups. Others, particularly ocean-living dolphins, may gather in their thousands. Dolphins are also found far up some great rivers in warmer parts of the world, such as the Amazon in South America and the Ganges, Indus and Yangtze rivers in Asia.

There are two main types of cetacean. Some, such as the blue whale, have special filters in their mouths, called baleen plates, to sieve food from the sea. Other cetaceans, such as the sperm whale, have teeth to catch their prey. Dolphins are toothed cetaceans, and this book will tell you about the life cycle of one of them – the bottlenose dolphin.

DOLPHIN ANCESTORS

All land animals evolved from animals that lived in the sea. However, more than 50 million years ago, a meat-eating wolf-like animal with hooves gave up its life on land and returned to the water. Over time, its shape changed to suit its new watery home. One result is the dolphin family, whose closest land relatives are hoofed animals such as cows. Some dolphins still have useless hind-leg bones under their skin.

A Dolphin is Born

A dolphin mother is ready to give birth about twelve months after mating. Some mothers prefer to give birth in the relative calm and safety of coastal waters, but many have their young, called calves, out in the open sea. Female bottlenose dolphins usually have only one calf. Twins are rare and unlikely to survive.

The young of mammals are usually born head-first, but a dolphin calf is normally born tail-first. The calf's tail flukes and dorsal fin are floppy, to make its birth easier. They soon become firm.

▲ A mother and her calf breathe together at the surface. A newborn calf finds breathing difficult at first, and has to take many more breaths than its mother.

▶ A dolphin calf swims through the waves with its mother. The calf is fully formed at birth and can swim straight away.

A CHILLING BIRTH

The unborn calf is cosy in its mother's womb at a constant temperature of 37°C, but the sea water outside is much colder. The new-born calf cannot afford to be shocked by this temperature difference, because it has to rush to the surface immediately and take its first breath. Its mother helps by urging the calf upwards with her head, beak or flippers.

The new-born dolphin calf may weigh as much as 20 kilograms and be over a metre long – more than one-third the length of its mother!

The calf feeds on its mother's milk about one hour after being born, then at least four times an hour after that. Although the calf doesn't yet have teeth to get in the way, its lack of flexible lips means it cannot suckle properly. So the mother squirts her milk into the calf's mouth.

Early Days

The bottlenose mother tries to protect her new calf, which is only interested in feeding as much as possible. To make feeding easier, the mother sometimes rolls her body on to its side. This means the calf doesn't have to swim underneath to reach the teats on her mammary glands.

For at least the first week, the mother and calf are never apart. During this time, she doesn't hunt. The calf saves energy by swimming close to her side, so it gets pulled along in her slipstream.

▶ Nourished by its mother's fat-rich milk, a young dolphin gains weight rapidly.

▼ Swimming at its mother's side may help to camouflage the young calf, making its shape less obvious to predators such as sharks and orcas.

10

DOLPHIN MILK

A dolphin mother's milk contains more than five times as much fat as human milk. The young calf feeds from both its mother's mammary glands, each of which has a single teat. The teats are hidden away in her belly until feeding time.

Apart from its small size, a new-born calf is easy to spot. It has paler than normal skin and may have vertical stripes, called foetal folds, on its body. The stripes are caused by the way the calf's large body is folded up in the womb before birth.

Some calves are born with whiskers on their beaks, but they usually lose them after a few weeks or months. The function of the whiskers is unclear, but they may be important for touch. Having whiskers may help the bottlenose calf to stay in close contact with its mother at night or in murky water.

Babysitting

The calf depends on its mother's milk for its first twelve to eighteen months. For the mother to feed herself and produce enough milk for her calf, she has to catch nearly one-tenth of her own body-weight in food each day. The calf is at risk from predators such as great white sharks or orcas if it is left alone while its mother goes off hunting.

Pregnant females and mothers with young calves usually travel together in groups, called bands. The females are often related and the close bonds between them encourage them to care for all the calves. They do this by taking turns babysitting the young calves while the others hunt.

▲ Great white sharks prey on unprotected bottlenose calves if they get the chance. Tight-knit bands of dolphins, in which all the females help to guard the young, may help to keep prowling sharks at bay.

▶ Groups of related females co-operate closely in looking after the calves. Males are thought to play no part in rearing the young dolphins.

12

'Midwife' dolphins may help with the birth of a new calf, biting through the umbilical cord between a mother and her calf. 'Aunt' dolphins guide the calf to the surface for its first breath, while 'nurses' suckle calves that are not their own. One female may act as aunt, midwife and nurse.

The young calf gradually becomes more and more adventurous. After just a few weeks, it starts to spend some time on its own.

WHISTLE YOUR NAME

Soon after birth, a mother whistles to her calf. At first the whistle is just a single, steady note. But it quickly develops into a complex sound, called a signature whistle. The calf will use this as its 'name' for the rest of its life. Older dolphins can copy these whistles and often mimic each other's calls.

Infanticide

One of the biggest dangers to many young mammals is a deadly attack by an adult of the same species. This is called infanticide.

Adult bottlenose dolphins sometimes kill harbour porpoises. Scientists have noticed that the dead porpoises have similar injuries to some dead bottlenose calves found on beaches. This may be evidence that infanticide is occurring, with bottlenose males killing calves.

Infanticide may occur because an adult male hopes that if he kills a calf, its mother will mate with him to get a new calf.

PROTECTING CALVES

A female bottlenose dolphin usually mates with several different males. This may help to protect her calf against infanticide. When the calf is born twelve months later, none of the males will be sure whether or not he is the father of her calf. If he kills the calf, he risks killing his own offspring.

◀ A young calf may be at risk from adult bottlenose males, as well as from predators. The males may kill porpoises to practise killing dolphin calves.

Even if infanticide does occur, there is no doubt that dolphin society is normally extremely protective. There are many records of dolphins helping not only fellow dolphins but also other species, including humans.

▼ A bottlenose dolphin has between 78 and 102 cone-shaped teeth. An adult may use its teeth to attack other cetaceans, leaving long scratch marks called rakes. The worst injuries occur when the dolphin uses its beak as a battering ram, or its tail as a club.

Growing Up

The relationship between a bottlenose dolphin mother and her calf may last for at least six years. Being together for so long allows the mother to teach the youngster about its habitat, where and how to find food, and how to behave towards other dolphins.

▼ Living with its mother in a band of females, the calf quickly learns about the relationships and rules that govern dolphin society.

A mother and an older calf touch beaks to reinforce social bonds. Even when it is independent, the calf will still be able to identify its mother in a large school by listening for her signature whistle.

Weaning begins at four months. Although the calf starts to eat solid food, such as fish or squid, it will usually carry on being suckled for at least another year. Sometimes, suckling continues for several years, perhaps to provide extra food in the calf's early independence, or to reinforce the bond between mother and calf.

Growth is rapid and by eighteen months old, the calf has doubled its length and quadrupled its weight. Early growth is important in all marine mammals, because the bigger or fatter the animal becomes, the less heat it will lose to the cold water around it.

World of Sound

Thanks to the weird and wonderful sounds dolphins make – from buzzes, squawks and clicks to yelps and pops – the dolphin calf grows up in a world that is never quiet.

Visibility underwater is bad, because light travels poorly in even the clearest waters. Sound, on the other hand, travels much faster and further in water than it does in air. To make the most of their aquatic home, dolphins have developed excellent hearing and the ability to use sound underwater.

◀ A dolphin has a tiny ear opening on each side of its head, just behind the eye. It may be that these ear openings can only hear sounds above the water's surface. Vital underwater sounds travel to the dolphin's inner ear through its jawbone, not through the outer ear openings.

Dolphins use click-like sounds mainly to hunt and explore their surroundings, and whistles, squeaks and other sounds to communicate. For example, they may 'blow' their signature whistles in different ways to mean different things. A dolphin may whistle 'I'm Bob ...', but by making its whistle louder or shorter, he may also be saying '... and I'm frightened.' It is possible that dolphins also use sounds to represent objects, such as fish.

Dolphins can also send signals by hitting their bodies against the water's surface. A belly-flop may be a greeting to dolphins far away, or a tail-slap may mean 'I'm angry, stay away.' Each may mean something different in a different situation.

▲ Nobody knows how dolphins make their clicking sounds, but they may use both their larynx (voice-box) and nasal passages (situated below the blowhole). The blowhole does not breathe out air while the dolphin is making its clicking sounds.

Family and Friends

Schools of bottlenose dolphins vary in size from a few individuals to several hundred. The largest gatherings are simply the coming together of many smaller groups made up of families, friends or temporary companions.

Aged between three and six years, the calf, now called a juvenile, becomes largely independent of its mother and has to find food for itself. By now the mother may be pregnant again or even have a new calf. She encourages her older calf's independence, but their relationship remains close. If a new calf dies, the older calf may even begin suckling again.

◀ Apart from a few close family members, a dolphin school may vary from day to day.

The juvenile slowly replaces its mother's company with that of other juveniles, many of whom were reared by the same band of females. The juveniles join sub-adult groups, which are usually either all-male 'bachelor' groups or mixed-sex groups. Occasionally, females form a 'girls-only' sub-adult group.

▼ Playing together is an important part of life in dolphin society. Groups of dolphins enjoy nothing better than surfing the waves.

Apart from the dangerous few weeks following birth, this early independence is the most difficult time in a dolphin's life. The pressures of building social status, avoiding predators and having to fend for themselves leads many to the brink of starvation. Sadly, the death toll is high.

Hunter and Hunted

During adolescence, young dolphins learn to use the knowledge of hunting given to them by their mothers and other band members. The young dolphins' choice of prey is important if they are to survive to adulthood. They must learn to avoid harmful species, such as the venomous scorpion fish or lionfish found in the Tropics.

Dolphins must also choose prey that provides lots of fat or protein, such as mackerel or mullet, for the least amount of hunting effort. There is no point using more energy to catch a fish than the fish contains. If a dolphin makes too many bad decisions, it will starve.

▼ Dolphins seem to be able to distinguish between fish that are nutritious and good to eat, such as these mullet, and those that provide so little nourishment they are not worth catching.

DOLPHIN FOOD CHAIN

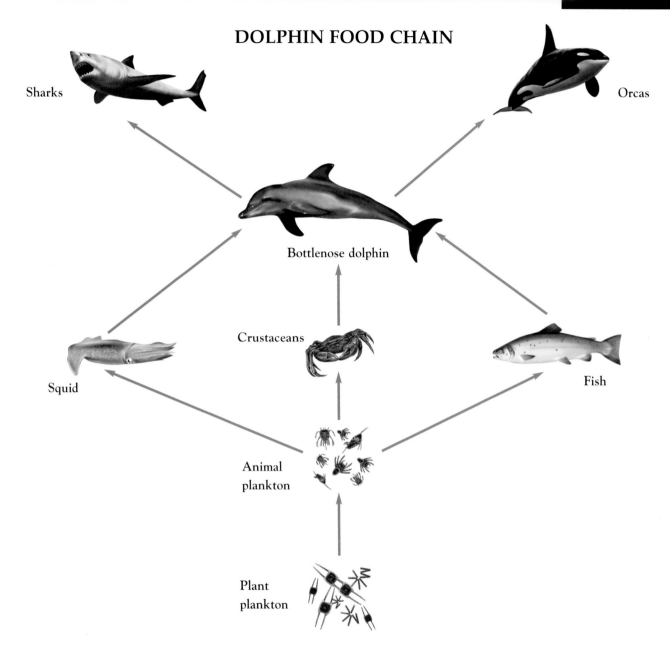

Sharks

Orcas

Bottlenose dolphin

Crustaceans

Squid

Fish

Animal plankton

Plant plankton

Adult dolphins are sometimes preyed upon by orcas and sharks, including the great white shark and the tiger shark. However, bottlenose dolphins are large compared to other dolphins, so these attacks are probably rare. Bottlenose dolphins may even sometimes attack sharks to drive them away.

▲ At the bottom of the bottlenose dolphin's food chain are tiny living things called plankton.

Seeing with Sound

Humans live in a world of light, so sight has become our most important sense. But because dolphins live in a murky, underwater world, they have developed a method of 'seeing' with sound. This amazing ability is called echolocation, and they use it to find food and to navigate.

The dolphin makes a pulse of sound called an echolocation click. It then waits for an echo to return. If it hears an echo, it knows that the click has bounced back off an object in the water. The longer the echo takes to return, the further away the object is. If the echo doesn't return, the dolphin knows there's nothing there.

▼ This cross-section of a dolphin's head shows where the clicks might be produced and how they are transmitted.

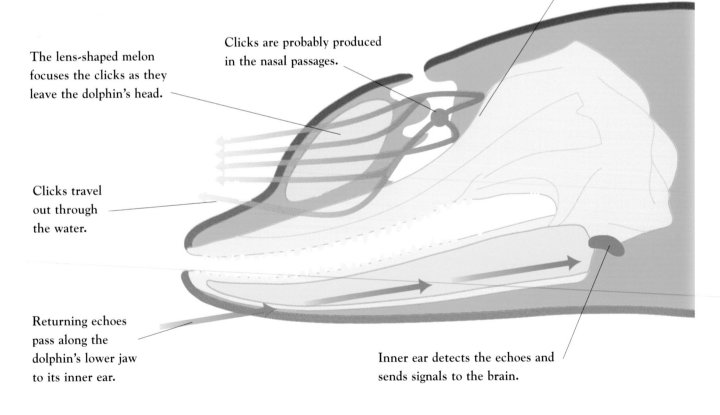

The dish-shaped skull also helps to focus the clicks.

The lens-shaped melon focuses the clicks as they leave the dolphin's head.

Clicks are probably produced in the nasal passages.

Clicks travel out through the water.

Returning echoes pass along the dolphin's lower jaw to its inner ear.

Inner ear detects the echoes and sends signals to the brain.

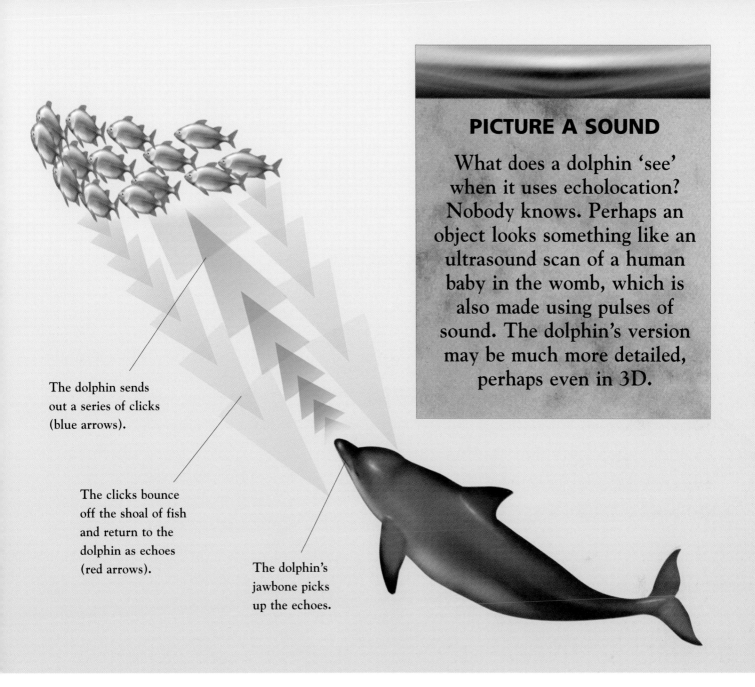

The dolphin sends out a series of clicks (blue arrows).

The clicks bounce off the shoal of fish and return to the dolphin as echoes (red arrows).

The dolphin's jawbone picks up the echoes.

PICTURE A SOUND

What does a dolphin 'see' when it uses echolocation? Nobody knows. Perhaps an object looks something like an ultrasound scan of a human baby in the womb, which is also made using pulses of sound. The dolphin's version may be much more detailed, perhaps even in 3D.

In reality, the dolphin's echolocation is probably much more complicated than this, and we can only guess at what information it provides. Hundreds of clicks can be made in a fraction of a second, detecting objects up to 100 metres away. Some scientists think that dolphins may be able to use powerful echolocation clicks to stun fish, or to tell whether a female dolphin is pregnant.

▲ Some parts of a fish's body return echoes better than others. So this dolphin may be seeing a shoal of body parts rather than whole fish.

Finding food

Bottlenose dolphins eat mainly fish and squid, which they catch with their pointed teeth. Occasionally they will eat crustaceans such as shrimps. Dolphins need to do a lot of hunting to survive – a 75 kilogram calf, for example, has to fill its stomach four or five times every day.

Bottlenose dolphins have even been seen teaming up with false killer whales (another type of dolphin) to attack sperm whales. Scientists are puzzled by this, because false killer whales also eat dolphins and dolphins can't eat sperm whales.

FISHING PALS

In Mauritania, the fishermen of the Imragen tribe are helped by bottlenose dolphins. The fishermen attract dolphins by hitting the water with sticks. The dolphins drive fish towards the shore, where other tribe members cast their nets to catch them. The advantage to the dolphins is that they find it easier to feed on the dense cluster of fish.

▲ These bottlenose dolphins are chasing a shoal of fish. The disturbance they create in the water helps to herd the fish closer together so they are easier to catch.

◄ Swimming together in shoals helps fish to reduce the chance of being the one that's eaten. It may also make it difficult for predators such as dolphins to pick out individual fish.

Dolphins often co-operate closely when hunting. Oceanic bottlenose dolphins herd fish together against the surface or into large fish 'balls', then each takes its turn to feed. In Carolina, USA, bottlenose dolphins herd fish close to the shore then rush at them. This creates a wave that washes the struggling fish on to the mud, closely followed by the dolphins, who nearly strand themselves.

Dolphins also feed individually and may dive to depths of over 500 metres. They chase fish by sight and echolocation, and can even find fish hidden beneath the sand. Dolphins can also flick fish clear of the water with their tails, stunning or killing their victims.

Adult Life

Bottlenose dolphins are probably the most widespread of all dolphins. They have adapted to live in many different habitats around the world and learned to catch and eat many different types of prey. Within its particular habitat, an adult dolphin has a home range. This is the area in which it spends most of its time.

▼ This adult bottlenose dolphin is blowing a trail of bubbles as it swims in its home range off the coast of Israel. A home range may cover hundreds or thousands of square kilometres.

▶ An adult dolphin's sleek, muscular body makes it an acrobatic swimmer, able to leap several metres into the air and reach speeds of up to 40 kilometres per hour in the water.

Adult bottlenose dolphins living in cold waters grow larger than those in warmer waters. This is because they need more blubber under their skin to keep them warm. Living in such different habitats may one day lead to cold and warm-water dolphins becoming separate species, unable to inter-breed.

Breeding age

Females become able to breed between the ages of five and thirteen, and males between nine and fifteen. Females that produce calves at an early age may not have the experience or a sufficiently well-developed body to rear their calves successfully. On average, females become sexually mature aged ten and males aged twelve. Both will not reach their full adult size until two or three years later.

Finding a Mate

More male bottlenose dolphins die in adolescence than females. No one is sure why this happens, but it means that when the dolphins mature and leave their sub-adult groups, there are fewer males than females.

Alone, or with a few friends of the same age, the males travel widely between female groups in search of opportunities to breed. At the same time, the newly matured females return to the maternal band in which they were born, living once again with sisters, mothers and even grandmothers.

▲ Two bottlenose dolphins mate at the water's surface.

▶ These large male bottlenose dolphins in Scotland's Cromarty Firth are fighting for the right to mate with a female.

Courtship is accompanied by yelps and may involve chases, jumping together out of the water, and lots of flipper contact. The dolphins usually mate in a belly-to-belly position. Male and female sexual organs are hidden away beneath slits along the belly. This is one reason why it's difficult to tell the sexes apart.

Both males and females may mate with many partners. Mature female bottlenose dolphins will usually have a calf every two to four years, giving birth mostly in late spring and early autumn.

COMPETITION

Males compete with each other – often violently – to be able to mate with females, which may be why males have shorter lives. An individual male, or a small male group, may separate a female from her band and guard her from other males for many days while mating with her. During this time, another male or male group may try to steal the female away.

Lifespan

Life for a dolphin is much tougher than most people think. Finding enough to eat, keeping warm, and avoiding accidents or attacks from other marine mammals and sharks takes a heavy toll on a dolphin's health.

If a bottlenose dolphin survives into adulthood, it may live to between twenty-five and thirty years old if it is male, and perhaps up to fifty if it is female. The three major natural causes of death are parasites, disease and predators.

STRANDED!

Cetaceans sometimes get stuck, or stranded, on beaches or sandbanks. This may be because their brains or senses have been affected by parasites, causing them to become confused. Alternatively, healthy animals may lose their way, fooled by unfamiliar coastal features. Some old or sick cetaceans may become stranded when they enter shallow waters for safety.

▲ When dolphins wash ashore dead, it is often hard to know why they died, unless there are obvious signs such as fishing-net or shark-bite marks.

◀ Tiger sharks are fearsome predators. This bottlenose dolphin was lucky to escape alive from an encounter with a tiger shark, as the scars in its back show.

Dolphins' bodies are home to many parasites, which are animals that live by feeding off other animals. These parasites include tapeworms, nematodes and flukes. They do not usually cause serious harm to the dolphin's health. But if a dolphin is ill or very old, the parasites can make it so weak that it dies.

Disease can spread rapidly among dolphins. In 1987, a virus killed at least 2,500 bottlenose dolphins off America's south-east coast. Sadly, there is evidence that many diseases are being made worse or even caused by pollution.

Dolphins and Humans

For centuries, sailors have thrilled to the sight of dolphins riding the bow-waves of ships, often no more than an arm's length away. Until recently, ancient tales of dolphins befriending humans were thought to be no more than 'tall tales' made up by seafarers.

Over the past fifty years, however, there have been many reports of individual dolphins settling in one area and seeking out human company. Most turn out to be male bottlenose dolphins. The dolphins, who love frolicking with swimmers, become local celebrities.

▼ Monkey Mia in Shark Bay, Australia, is home to several hundred bottlenose dolphins. Some of these, usually small family groups, have been coming to the beach to 'meet the humans' since the late 1960s. The females trust humans enough to bring their young calves with them.

No one is sure whether these dolphins are orphans or whether they are alone because they have been thrown out of their social group. Perhaps they are just curious dolphins who investigated a place and then settled there because it met all their needs.

Bottlenose dolphins, orcas and other cetaceans are sometimes taken from the ocean and kept in zoos. Many people now believe that such captivity is cruel, because captive animals suffer from stress, behavioural problems and shorter lifespans. We can learn much more about cetaceans by watching them in the wild instead of zoos.

▶ This captive orca is performing in a zoo.

Brain Power

In the 1960s, the American space agency NASA began to study dolphin 'language' to find out how easy it might be to talk to aliens. Sadly, no two-way conversation ever took place with dolphins, but this work did reveal much about dolphins' brain power.

A dolphin calf's brain weighs 0.8 kilograms at birth, and continues to develop until the age of nine or ten – much longer than in most other mammals. This is a sign that learning over a long period is important to dolphins, just as it is to humans.

▲ A researcher uses hand signals to communicate with captive dolphins.

◄ Are dolphins clever? Some of the things that dolphins do suggest that they may be very intelligent. Dolphins have learned to use sponges to protect their beaks from sharp objects when hunting on coral reefs. They have also been known to skillfully unpick fishing nets.

An adult dolphin's brain weighs approximately 2 kilograms. Compared to its overall body-weight, a dolphin brain is only slightly smaller than a human brain. The dolphin may need such a large brain to cope with its complex social life and senses, such as echolocation.

Research has shown that dolphins can use sounds to pass information to each other. They can also understand simple instructions. A dolphin can even be taught the difference between 'take the ball to the hoop' and 'take the hoop to the ball'. But because dolphins live in such a different environment to our own, the question 'are dolphins intelligent?' may never be answered.

Threats

Although the bottlenose dolphin itself is not at risk, human activities have put a number of cetacean species in danger of extinction. These include the Yangtze river dolphin, the Gulf of California porpoise and the Northern right whale. Only a few hundred of each species are left.

Dolphins face different threats depending on where they live. The habitat of river dolphins, for example, is being changed by farming and large dams. Some dolphins are injured by collisions with river boats and others are caught in nets, or poisoned by chemical waste dumped in rivers.

▼ A dolphin hitches a free ride on the bow-wave produced by a huge ship, but the noise of the ship's engines may end up harming the dolphin.

In some countries, dolphins are killed either for food or because local fishermen mistakenly believe they scare fish away from the waters where they take their catch. Even where they are protected, visits from well-meaning 'dolphin watchers' can upset the lifestyle of wild dolphins.

Loud noises from oil exploration at sea, commercial shipping and naval vessels may also be harmful. This 'noise pollution' may alter the dolphins' behaviour, perhaps even affecting their ability to hear. A further unmeasurable threat to cetaceans and other sea creatures is posed by global warming, which could change ocean temperatures and permanently alter the Earth's weather.

▶ Oil and gas rigs can pollute the oceans by leaking or dumping toxic chemicals into the water.

Pollution and Fishing

Many polluting chemicals dumped in the oceans are absorbed by tiny marine animals at the bottom of the food chain. They become more concentrated in animals further up the chain.

By eating other marine animals, dolphins receive highly concentrated amounts of pollutants that mainly end up being stored in their blubber. When a dolphin is sick or producing milk, it breaks down blubber to provide extra energy. But this also frees the pollutants, which can damage the dolphin's fertility and its ability to fight diseases. A mother passes huge quantities of these pollutants to her calf through her milk.

▲ For all their amazing abilities, wild dolphins can't swim backwards: if they get caught in a net, there's no way out.

▶ Fishing vessels, such as this trawler, catch over 100 million tonnes of sea-life each year – more than the sea can naturally replace. Dwindling populations of sea creatures will reduce the food available to cetaceans, and may threaten their survival.

TUNA FISHING

Over the last 30 years, 7 million dolphins have been killed by tuna fishing in the eastern Pacific Ocean. Yellowfin tuna often swim below schools of dolphins. The tuna fishermen know that if they net the dolphins, they are likely to catch the tuna as well. Consumers can help dolphins by buying 'dolphin-friendly' tuna. This has been caught with fishing lines rather than nets, so it causes less harm to dolphins.

Fishing is another danger. Each year, many thousands of dolphins and porpoises die when they get entangled in fishing nets. Some nets, such as drift nets, are difficult for dolphins to see. Others, such as trawl nets, may be used in such a way that dolphins can't avoid them.

Protection

In the late 1960s, the 'Save the Whale' campaign made people aware of just how many whales were being hunted and how cruel the hunting methods were. The public then discovered that large numbers of dolphins were dying in US tuna nets. The result was the 1972 Marine Mammal Protection Act, which has done much to protect marine mammals in US waters and beyond. Since then, several other countries have also introduced laws to preserve marine mammals and their habitats.

▼ Educational dolphin and whale-watching trips allow many people to enjoy the sight of cetaceans in the wild. Conservationists are drawing up guidelines to try and ensure that such trips disturb the animals as little as possible.

▲ Two bottlenose dolphins leap gracefully through the air. As scientists and conservationists learn more about the lives of these intelligent, beautiful creatures, we will also learn how to protect them better.

Fortunately, pollution is slowly being reduced and stricter controls are being placed on fishing. A number of international agreements on pollution and fishing are now in force or are in the process of being set up.

You can find out about organizations working to save dolphins and other cetaceans on page 47.

Dolphin Life Cycle

 Following a twelve-month pregnancy, a dolphin mother usually gives birth to a single calf. The calf is able to swim straight away, and sometimes has to drink its mother's milk on the move.

2 For the first week, the mother and calf are inseparable. The calf soon begins to swim on its own. It is looked after by female relatives while its mother goes off hunting.

 Weaning begins as early as four months, but the calf carries on drinking milk until it is eighteen months old. The bond between mother and calf will be strong for several years.

4   Between three and six years of age, the juvenile dolphin leaves its maternal band. It joins a sub-adult group, which includes the friends it has grown up with.

5   Females mature between five and thirteen years old, but males mature later, at about the age of twelve. The females return to the bands in which they were born. Males go off in search of females with whom they can breed.

6   Females have a calf every two to four years and may continue to breed into their forties. Females may live for up to fifty years. Males usually only reach their early thirties, perhaps because of violent clashes with rival males.

GEOGRAPHY

- Mapwork: where dolphins live.
- Water: rivers and coasts.
- Environmental change: global warming and sea-level changes.
- Tourism: dolphin watching.
- Food journeys.

ART

- Shape and movement.
- Water in art.

SCIENCE

- Ocean and river habitats.
- Classification: mammals and cetaceans.
- Adaptation: dolphin's body shape.
- Dolphin's life cycle.
- Food chain and pollution.
- Protection of the marine environment.

Dolphin Topic Web

MATHS

- Dolphin numbers.
- Height and weight comparisons.
- Compare the energy value of different prey.

ICT

- Look at conservation groups' websites.
- Send an email to the government expressing a point of view.

ENGLISH & LITERACY

- Dolphin myths and legends.
- Write a story about a day in the life of a dolphin.
- Conservation debates.

Extension Activities

English
- Role play and debate: assign roles and debate the conflict between fishermen and dolphin conservationists.
- Find and list collective names for groups of animals (e.g. school, herd, pod) or terms for their young.

Maths
- Compare the numbers of cetaceans around the world e.g. dolphins compared to orcas.

Geography
- Trace a world map from an atlas. Colour and label the major seas and oceans.
- Make a dolphin distribution map, including river and ocean dolphins.
- Trace the journey of tuna fish from the seas to the supermarket.

Science
- Compare human and dolphin body parts. Make links between parts that have the same function.
- Discuss the effect of squid overfishing on dolphins.

46

Glossary

Adolescence The period between being a young animal and an adult.

Blubber A layer of fat under a dolphin's skin that keeps it warm.

Cetacean A dolphin, porpoise or whale.

Courtship Behaviour that leads to mating.

Crustaceans A group of animals with a hard outer body casing and jointed limbs.

Echolocation The way dolphins use sound to locate prey and find their way around.

Evolved Developed slowly over time.

Extinction The dying out of a species.

Global warming The gradual warming of the Earth's climate caused by pollution.

Habitat The natural home of a species.

Infanticide The killing of young animals by older members of the same species.

Mammals Warm-blooded animals that produce milk for their young.

Mammary gland Part of a female mammal's body that produces milk.

Parasites Animals or plants that live in or on another animal and feed off it.

Pollution Spoiling the environment with harmful chemicals and gases (pollutants).

Predator An animal that hunts and kills other animals (called prey) for food.

Slipstream The current of water produced by a boat or swimming animal.

Social status An animal's rank, or level of importance, within a group.

Species A group of animals or plants that are able to breed with one another.

Suckle To suck milk from a mother's teats.

Umbilical cord The tube that connects a mammal mother to her unborn baby.

Weaning The time when a calf stops drinking milk and starts eating solid food.

Further Information

Organisations to Contact

WWF-UK
Panda House, Weyside Park
Godalming, Surrey GU7 1XR
Tel: 01483 426444
Website: www.wwf-uk.org

Whale and Dolphin
Conservation Society
Alexander House, James Street
West, Bath BA1 2BT
Tel: 01225 334511
Website: www.wdcs.org

Websites

Kids CARE About Whales
http://whales.magna.com.au/KIDS/
News and photos about whale and dolphin conservation, and the chance to air your views.

The Whale Club
http://www.whaleclub.com/
A site for people keen to help marine mammals, with pictures, information and a gift shop.

Books to Read

Dolphins and Porpoises by Janelle Hatherly and Delia Nichols (Facts On File, 1992)
Nature Watch: Whales and Dolphins by Robin Kerrod (Lorenz, 1998)
Whale by Vassili Papastravou (Dorling Kindersley Eyewitness Guides, 1993)
Whales, Dolphins and Porpoises by Mark Carwardine (Dorling Kindersley, 1992)

Index

Page numbers in **bold** refer to photographs or illustrations.